BOVEY TRACEY

REDISCOVERED

To Terry

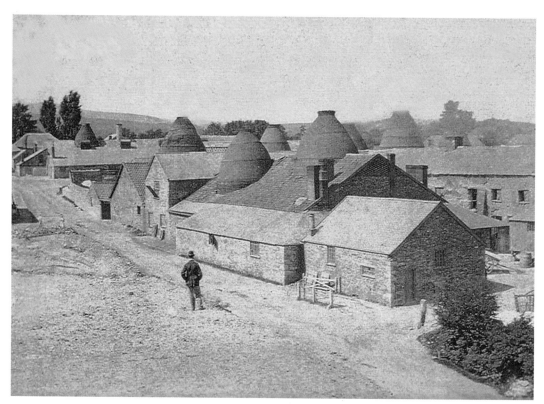

A rare postcard giving a general view across Bovey Tracey Pottery from the 1890 - 1900s. In 1895 a limited company was formed with the directors of the Bristol Pottery who took on responsibility for the new Bovey Pottery Company Ltd. The view shows very old kilns, one dating back to 1810. Note the small weigh-bridge next to the hut on the right. The building on staddle stones on the far right was the grain store. The grain was used to feed the horses that pulled the carts around the pottery. The photographer was F. Bedford who was the photographer to the Prince of Wales.

BOVEY TRACEY REDISCOVERED

Elizabeth Westwood

Coombe Meadow Publishing

Joan Mann, Arthur Mann's sister, having a ride on the elephant in the early 1930s in Union Square. The circus came to Bovey each year and was held in a meadow at the end of Avenue Road, near the railway line. When the circus came to town, the elephants always used to stop at the bakers on Dolphin Square and the baker would come out as they went past and give them buns! They would then come up and drink at the Jubilee Fountain to wash them down!

© Elizabeth Westwood

First published 2012.

Coombe Meadow Publishing
Hilltop, Coombe Meadow
Bovey Tracey, Devon. TQ13 9EZ

British Library Cataloguing in Publication data.

A catalogue for this book is available from the British Library.

ISBN: 978-0-9573039-0-4

Typesetting, printing and binding by Wotton Printers.
Unit 5, Riverside 2, Quay Road, Brunel Industrial Estate, Newton Abbot, Devon TQ12 4DZ

CONTENTS

Front cover: Girl in Union Square Bovey Tracey in 1908.
Back cover: Mr Henry Raisey with his flock of sheep and sheepdog going from the bluebell woods at Lustleigh towards Southbrook Farm in the 1940s.

College Cottages looking towards the Parish Church in 1895. The families in this early photograph are named as Rich, Heath, Lethbridge and Holmes. Known as 'College' these houses were rebuilt in the 1950s. The cottages on the north side of the road opposite were demolished around 1895 to make way for the Courtenay Memorial. The rare early view was given to the Church by Mrs A. Cann, of 3 Alms Houses, Mary Street and was recently rediscovered in the organ loft at the Parish Church St Peter, St Paul and St Thomas of Canterbury Bovey Tracey.

INTRODUCTION

Bovey Tracey, originally known as South Bovey, is a small town situated in a lovely position on the eastern edge of Dartmoor National Park, home of the sturdy Dartmoor Pony. The River Bovey runs through the town and it is surrounded by beautiful countryside and farmland and within easy reach of the South Devon Coast. The population has expanded significantly over the last 200 years and Bovey and the surrounding area has become a very popular place to live with close links to Exeter and Plymouth and the proximity to Dartmoor being a great attraction.

At first glance visitors or people who have recently moved to Bovey Tracey may not know the rich and diverse history that the town and local area holds. The street names soon give plenty of clues, Pottery Road and Kiln Close, Station Road, Abbey Road, Battle Road and many more. This fascinating selection of late nineteenth and early twentieth century postcards and photographs soon makes us realise how life today has changed dramatically and it is now hard to imagine Bovey as it used to be.

As life continues to change at such a fast pace, it is good to look back sometimes at our great heritage and remember the past. This book provides the opportunity to rediscover and capture again a sense of some of those earlier times, the pictures speak for themselves. Bovey Tracey has always been a town of great character and interest and it remains a very special place today.

It has been a most enjoyable time gathering the images and information for this book and I hope that readers will get as much pleasure from it as I have had in its compilation.

An early photograph from the 1890s of children in Union Square, Bovey Tracey.

ACKNOWLEDGEMENTS

Collecting things has always been a passion and over recent years since moving to the area, an interest in collecting local pottery led to my husband and I also collecting local postcards and photographs of Bovey Tracey. Through collecting and in compiling this book, I have learned so much about the fascinating and rich local history of Bovey Tracey and Heathfield and I would like to thank all my Bovey friends for their interest and support.

I would like to acknowledge all who have written on the history of Bovey before and hope this book will help to complement previous publications and make a small contribution to further preserving local knowledge and heritage of the area.

In particular I would like to thank the following: Terry for all his love, support and scanning!

Carole and Peter Hammond without whose encouragement, advice and great expertise this book would not have been published.

With very special thanks to Mr Dave Lewis, for allowing us to use some of his collection and for sharing his memories of Bovey past.

Mike Lang for his help with the railway captions. For further information see 'The Newton Abbot to Moretonhampstead Railway' by Anthony R. Kingdom & Mike Lang, ARK publications 2004.

Viv Styles for her great help and enthusiasm in researching some of the caption information and pictures

John Morris for sharing his unique early photograph collection.

Bovey Tracey Heritage Centre.

Brian Adams, Jean Brothwood, Dawn Carrington, Francis Chudley, Pat Collins, Julie Dyer, Christine Gale, Rev. Graham Hamilton, Kevin Hooke, Noel and Loui Lavis, Arthur and Helen Mann, John Midgley, May Moir, Jackie Parkinson, Mary Parry, Hedley and Marion Upham, David Wedden.

St Catherine's School, Heathfield.

The staff of Wotton Printers for all their help.

In the case of some photos it has not been possible to identify the copyright holder so my apologies if anyone's copyright has been infringed.

CHAPTER 1

SHOPS

Right up to the time of the Second World War there was no need to travel anywhere to shop as there were numerous shops and shopkeepers in Bovey that supplied your every need, from saddles and shoes to hats and underwear! There used to be eight grocers, three greengrocers, six garages, three butchers, three bakers, three dress shops, two newsagents, six dairymen and four hairdressers - two for ladies and two for gentlemen! There was even a shop offering umbrella repairs!

Richard Samuel Ladd, bookseller and fancy stationer, agent for Royal Insurance Company, stamp distributor and postmaster, Fore Street, with his wife, Alice Grebel and boys. This early photograph was taken around 1900. The building is now the Rowcroft shop.

The wholesale and retail ironmongers, Cummings Brothers, Town Hall Place, is the first shop on the left and is now Arnolds. The passageway seen on the left by the lamp post led to the forge and Jim Payne the blacksmith worked there into his eighties.

W.H. Tregoning, family grocers and provision merchants at Town Hall Place in 1922. Lance Tregoning is the boy in the picture. Before this it was Tom Cann's the photographer's shop and later the British Monument Café. It is where the Chinese takeaway is now.

The Co-operative Society shop stood at the beginning of East Street, where it joins Town Hall Place. It is now demolished and replaced by flats known as Pound Place. Reset into the wall of this modern building is a listed granite plaque dated from around the 1650s.

Star Supply Stores and staff at Town Hall Place. This is the same building as the above earlier view, but with a change of ownership. I wonder what the 'Free Gift' advertised in the window was? Next door, opposite the Front House Lodge was the Pound house and then two cottages.

Brinicombe's was a fruit and vegetable shop and is where the Fruit Shop is now at the top of Fore Street. The people in the photograph are in fancy dress and you can just see a poster advertising the Carnival on the door.

S. Gale, Milliner was situated on Fore Street on the corner of Orchard Terrace. The shop was later taken over by Cottles, a drapers. It then became the labour exchange. It was then Harris's shoe shop and is now the charity shop 'Animals in Distress'.

Harris's Reliable Footwear shop at 67 Fore Street. Marjorie Harris is in the doorway with one of her sons in the 1930s. In the Second World War a bomb dropped near Devon House and all the windows down this side of Fore Street were blown out and the rafters on this house were damaged.

View from Union Square dated 1934 looking up Fore St. 'R.G. Hodge' Ladies and Gent's hairdressers and tobacconist is on the left which was previously the post office. The building is now used by the Rowcroft shop.

Percy Peters and Sons, Off Licence shop, Fore Street. Note the advert for 'Wincarnis the Great Tonic.' This tonic wine was first produced in 1887 and is a blend of enriched wine and malt extract with a unique infusion of therapeutic herbs and spices and is still available today!

Mr P. W. Peters with his van outside his 'Peters' Stores' warehouse which was off Abbey Close near to where the library is now. Mr Peters also owned the Bovey Stores which was next to Sercombe's the saddlers on Union Square.

Mann's butchers shop in around 1900. Mr William Mann, Arthur Mann's great grandfather is the man with the bowler hat. Mr Mitchell is standing next to him, he was the slaughter man. The lady with the two children is a nursemaid. Now Mann's Delicatessen, it is the only shop in Bovey to retain its original name.

Mardon and Sons family grocers and provision merchants known as the 'Bee - Hive Stores' on Fore Street, and Uphams hairdressers in the early twentieth century. Opposite, Leonard Mardon ran a plumbing business and he was also in charge of the Fire Brigade.

William Sercombe's saddlery shop was on the corner of Union Square and Abbey Road where Lloyds the chemist is now. At one time over 100 horses were used in Bovey for carriage rides to Dartmoor. The shop was demolished in the 1930s and rebuilt as Collins garage and cycle shop.

A. E. Collins cycles and motors shop in the early twentieth century with Nancy Collins in the doorway.

Sam Tolley butcher's was next to where the Youth Café is now at the lower end of Fore Street. The shop stood next door to Webber's. The business closed in 1947 and other butchers then ran the shop. The building is now used by the Kingsteignton Veterinary Group.

Webber's groceries was situated at the corner of South View on lower Fore Street. Mr Webber used to smoke and the ash would sometimes fall on the meat and at one time the cat used to sleep on the bacon! Known more recently as 'Pixie Corner,' it is now the Youth Café.

Arthur Mitchell's butchers shop with staff and delivery bicycles! Eli Lang took over until the early 1950s. This shop on Station Road is where Todd's the butchers is now.

W. R. Thomas and Sons bakers, on Dolphin Square with May and Phyllis, Mr Thomas's daughters standing outside the shop. Originally the shop was run by Leakers who also owned Brinicombes at one time. The shop is still a bakery to this day.

CHAPTER 2

WORKING AND RURAL LIFE

The local significant clay deposits made Bovey Tracey an ideal site for pottery production. The Bovey Tracey Potteries began in the 1750s and for around 200 years provided employment to many local people. Three bottle kilns can still be seen at the main site at Bovey Heathfield on Pottery Road - now House of Marbles and Pottery Museum. Research has shown that as well as some very ordinary, naive and even coarse pottery, some high quality and intricately made wares were also made such as tea canisters.

Farming and agriculture has experienced tremendous changes over the last century, as have many other parts of working and rural life as some of the early pictures in this chapter show.

Men at the Bovey Pottery in the 1930s unloading a biscuit kiln, lifting out the heavy saggers loaded with pottery. A sagger was a clay box used for containing ware in a kiln. Note the special caps used to cushion the heavy sagger when it was placed on their heads. It must have been hard work as some kilns took several hundreds of saggers which needed to be loaded, stacked inside the kiln and then unloaded after firing.

The Pottery, Bovey Tracey.

A postcard with a general view of Bovey Tracey Pottery, dated 1912. There is a large 'brick kiln' to the right of the picture and in the foreground is the internal pottery tramway track.

Women working at Bovey Pottery inspecting a large collection of mugs and other items in 1935. The Bovey Pottery sadly closed in 1957 and 200 years of pottery production in Bovey Tracey ended.

Bovey Sawmills at New Park in around 1900. New Park is located off Pottery Road on the Ashburton Road. Nearby is 'Blue Waters' which originally was a clay and lignite (brown coal) pit opened by Lord William Courtenay in around 1750.

A
Weaver
at
Work

BOVEY
HANDLOOM
WEAVERS

Bovey Tracey
Devon

Bovey Handloom Weavers at 1, Station Road, was established by Angus Litster in 1938 and is still flourishing today. Apprenticed in the woollen mills of Galashiels he moved to Bovey and started weaving on an old handloom brought from his native Scotland which is still in use.

A steam engine threshing at harvest time in Bovey Tracey in the early twentieth century.

An early photograph of Southbrook Farm, off Southbrook Lane which originally led up to Attway Farm. It was part of the 'Hole estate' and was a dairy and arable farm. The railway cut through the middle of the farm.

Ploughing with oxen at Wifford Farm. Apparently named by the Saxons because beavers made a dam here which led to a shallow, safe crossing point or 'Wide Ford' or Wifford. Wifford Farm is off Pottery Road roundabout close to Old Newton Road and used to be a piggery.

An early photograph of Southbrook cottages. There were three cottages originally. In the farmyard opposite was a barn which contained the cider press. In the 1950s the buildings were empty and were used to store apples from the large orchards nearby.

Attway cottages and farm c.1525 were on the old pack horse trail from Parke to Hennock. The farm was divided into Lower and Higher Attway and its fields stretched down to the river and across towards Southbrook Farm. In 1971, the nearby land was sold for a vineyard and houses.

An early photograph of Five Wyches which is situated on the Haytor Road. Originally a farm it was owned by Arthur Jarvis who had several farms. He had a land army girl to help him during the Second World War.

R. E. Glanville and Sons' display of agricultural equipment. Glanville's was close to the railway station and farm implements were delivered by rail. It was situated where Jeffreys is now on St John's Lane.

Bowden's in the early twentieth century. This was situated behind the Town Hall at Town Hall Place and was a blacksmith's run by two brothers. They were one of the first firms in the area to produce ploughs.

A J Wyatt & Bruce's Bovey Roller Mills stood at the end of Station Road off St John's Lane and close to the railway level crossing. The factory burnt down in 1925 and was sold to Bruce's who later owned Challabrook Farm. The building on the left is still there and is now called Mill House and used by the Moorgate Veterinary Group.

Charlie Wills and Les Wyatt with a van loaded with sacks of meat meal with an advert for Molassine dog cakes on the back!

Wyatt and Bruce's lorry at the Bovey Roller Mills and driver Gilbert Hookway with his cup for Lorry Driver of the Year in the 1960s. The drivers delivered animal feed to most of Devon and Cornwall. The Mill was taken over by Bibby's in the 1990s and sold only a few years later.

An early picture of a steam roller and workers laying one of the first road surfaces over Bovey Bridge in the early 1900s.

Workmen outside the Bell Inn at Town Hall Place in the early twentieth century digging a trench with a foreman watching. There were no mechanical tools in those days!

Workmen standing next to the Bovey Bridge. The bridge was built in 1642 and was one of the main objectives for the Roundhead forces to capture in the battle of Bovey Heath in 1646.

CHAPTER 3

CHURCHES AND RELIGIOUS LIFE

Bovey has a rich ecclesiastical history. The number of churches of various denominations and the different styles of church buildings demonstrate religious development in the town. Bovey also has a number of other buildings that used to be associated with religious life such as the Mission House, 'College,' St John's cottages and The Devon House of Mercy.

The Town Cross originally stood on what was the old village green before being moved to its current position when the Town Hall was built in 1866. It was supposedly given by Matilda de Tracey in 1260 at the time the town was given borough status. It became a war memorial following the First World War. Remembrance Day each year is marked by people from the town standing here for the two minutes silence to pay their respects.

The Parish Church of St Peter, St Paul and St Thomas of Canterbury. Sir Henry de Tracey, the first Lord of the Manor is said to have erected the current building during the 13th century following the murder of Thomas Becket in 1170 by his ancestor Sir William de Tracey.

An interior view of the Parish Church before the installation of the organ in the 1880s with the font in the foreground. The beautiful chancel rood screen in St Peter, St Paul and St Thomas Church dates from the early fifteenth century. The pulpit is carved of stone and richly decorated.

St Peter, St Paul and St Thomas Church choir in 1951 with Reverend Owen Duxbury. There is a loyal band of bell ringers who still ring the bells weekly. In 2012, a special peal was rung for Queen Elizabeth II's Diamond Jubilee.

Old Church Cottage, Bovey Tracey.   Cann, Photo.

Old Church Cottage built in about 1490, is situated to the right of the main driveway at the entrance to the Parish Church on East Street. It was used for church meetings, meals and brewing of ale. It was sold by the Church in 1580 for financial reasons.

A unique early photographic view towards Coombe Cross showing College Cottages on both sides of the road dating from the 1890s. 'College' consisted of rows of thatched cottages built in the early fifteenth century. Members of the church choir, servers and clerks lived there.

College Cottages, Bovey Tracey.

Cann, Photo.

This view shows College Cottages on the south side of the road. The northern part had been demolished in 1896 for the building of the 'Courtenay Memorial,' which is behind the wall and railings seen on the right hand side of the picture. South College was rebuilt in the 1950s.

Mothers Union members meeting outside St Peter St Paul and St Thomas's Church Rooms in 1917. This Christian organisation was founded in 1876, and local records show that it started in Bovey Tracey in 1898. Meetings still take place here on a monthly basis.

'Grey Gables' on Bradley Road, formerly the vicarage (despite the postcard caption) for St Peter, St Paul and St Thomas Church was rebuilt in the early 1850s for the Reverend Honourable Charles Leslie Courtenay at a cost of £1,549. It still has a private chapel.

Devon House of Mercy, Bovey Tracey.

Devon House of Mercy was built in 1867 and was in use until 1940. This Victorian institution under the care of the Clewer Sisterhood, was set up to help destitute women gain a training so they could get employment in domestic service. Now known as 'Devon House' it has been converted into flats.

The interior of the large and ornate Chapel at the Devon House of Mercy. The inmates were referred to as 'penitents' or 'fallen' women in need of moral correction. Some learned needlework, and others worked in the laundry, kitchens or did housework.

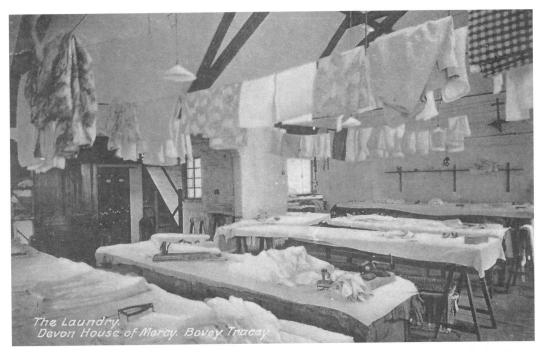

The women at Devon House of Mercy also took in washing from the town. This view shows the large ironing room. There was also a wash house which contained two large coppers and a very hot drying room. The 'infirmary cottage' was built in the grounds in 1878 in case of infection.

Located at the top of Devon House Drive, near to Devon House, this large detached red brick building was the priest's house for Devon House of Mercy. In around 1938 the priest was Rev Vandeberg. It is now called Hobland House and is one of Bovey's many listed buildings.

Cromwell Arch, Bovey Tracey

The Baptist Chapel at the top of the hill opened for worship in 1824. In the foreground of this postcard is an arch which was originally part of a twelfth century priory. Known locally as Cromwell's Arch, it is said to relate to when Oliver Cromwell came to Bovey Tracey in 1646 for the Battle of Bovey Heath.

The interior of the Baptist Chapel with the splendid organ which was removed in the 1990s. The pillars support an upper gallery, part of which is still in use. The Baptistry is under the floor in front of where the stage is now and the pews have been replaced with chairs.

MEMBERS OF THE UNION HOTEL'S BIBLE CLASS, Bovey Tracey, 3 September 1947.

Members of the Union Hotel's Bible class in September 1947, outside the Baptist Church. Bible study and then a beer!

The Temperance Hall was built on the west side of Lower Fore Street in 1877 for £600. In 1841 a local public meeting advocated 'the noble cause of total abstinence from every beverage of an intoxicating nature'! It was where 'Ashley Dawes' is now on Lower Fore Street.

A unique early photograph of nuns outside the Mission House on Upper Fore St, which was opened in 1879 at the instigation of Canon Courtenay. It originally had its own chapel. It is now a café known as Courtenay House or 'Pinks Place.'

An early photograph of a Sister from the Mission House with local girls. The nuns were from an Anglican order of the Convent of St John the Baptist, known as the Clewer Sisterhood. The sisters provided religious teaching, nursed the sick and helped the poor locally.

The Mary Street Methodist Chapel was built in 1880. Before this from 1806 worship took place in a nearby cottage. In 1967 the chapel closed and the congregation moved to the Congregational Church on Fore Street. Opposite is the British School now the Gospel Hall.

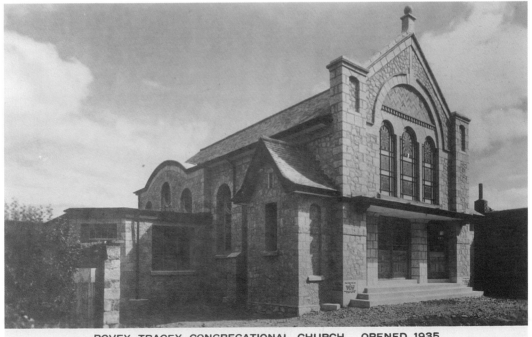

BOVEY TRACEY CONGREGATIONAL CHURCH. OPENED 1935

The Congregational Church, now the Methodist Church, was built in 1934. Most of the stained glass windows were commissioned by the Heath family. The organ, now removed, used to be positioned high up on a balcony at the front of the Church.

Church of the Holy Ghost, Bovey Tracey.

In 1904 a little Catholic chapel of the Holy Ghost made of corrugated iron sheets and lined with wood was erected on land rented from Squire Bentinck of Indio on the Ashburton Road opposite Moor View. Before this, Catholics in Bovey had to travel to Ugbrooke Chapel in Chudleigh!

CHURCH of the HOLY GHOST BOVEY TRACEY 11297

The interior of the 'Tin' church of the Holy Ghost. Following construction of the new church in 1936 the old church was used as a parish hall and became a temporary school for evacuee children during the Second World War and was then later demolished.

The Holy Spirit Catholic Church was consecrated in 1936. After the war, nuns and girls from Ingsdon Convent and Polish people from the nearby Stover camp for internees, dressed in their national costume, joined in their church processions.

The Interior of the Holy Spirit Catholic Church, Ashburton Road, Bovey Tracey around 1950. The presbytery is built next to the Church.

The Parish Church of St John the Evangelist was built as a chapel of ease in 1853. Charles Leslie Courtenay was appointed as vicar of Bovey Tracey in 1849, he married Lady Caroline Summers in the same year, who was Maid of Honour to Queen Victoria.

Interior of St John's Church. The reredos at the high altar depicts the Nativity, Resurrection and the Ascension. Rev. C. L. Courtenay served from 1849 to 1897 and became Canon of Windsor in 1857.

Bovey Tracey, St.John's Cottages

St John's cottages on Newton Road were built in the 1850s. There are few records, but it is known that the curate, the school mistress, organist and choirmaster of St John's Church lived there. Some interesting wall paintings were recently found in the sitting room of No 1.

St. John's Vicarage, Bovey Tracey.
Published by T. Cann, Bovey Tracey.

The St John's clergy house, later the vicarage, built at the end of 1851. This postcard with St John's Church in the background shows Rev Henry Martyn Wickham in the garden. Appointed in1895 he served as vicar for 40 years.

THE SISTERS' MONUMENT, BOVEY TRACEY   Fredman's Series

The Sisters' Monument, St John's churchyard. The three local Gurney sisters were on holiday in Egypt with their brother when a tragedy occurred. They left Boulac the port of Cairo on the 19th December 1876 and were travelling up the Nile on a dehabiah (a passenger sailing vessel) called the Aurora when on the evening of 23rd December the vessel capsized in bad weather and sadly the sisters were drowned. They lived at St John's villa, Bovey Tracey. Rev Fredrick Gurney their brother was curate to Bovey Tracey in 1871 and the current St John's pulpit was given in his memory in 1898.

CHAPTER 4

CELEBRATIONS AND LEISURE

The Bovey Tracey Carnival celebrations have taken place annually for over a century. The carnival is a popular event and a chance for everyone to dress up and have some fun as well as raise money for local charities. Leisure and sporting activities still play an important part in local life today just as in these early postcards and photographs.

Ken Harris and Don Hassall, members of the South Devon Vespa Club, at Orchard Way in 1956, with the cup which they won following a competition in France. They had to transport a box of large headed white chrysanthemums over long distances around France staying in hotels each night. The team that won was the one who had managed to keep the flowers in the best condition at the end of the race near Monte Carlo! The local Vespa Club headquarters was at 64 Fore Street, Bovey Tracey. This was where Ken Harris had a scooter shop.

This is the earliest Bovey Tracey carnival photograph, dated 1910. Can you imagine more dismal looking clowns? Perhaps they were afraid to smile in case their make-up cracked! Notice the Union Jacks decorating the float with portraits of the new King George V and Queen Mary.

A band of clowns and a pirate outside Union Hotel, Union Square, ready for the carnival.

' Tea for Two,' carnival entry at Town Hall Place parked just behind the Town Hall.

Bovey Pottery Pond Naval Band and their carnival float in the early 1900s.

The Bovey Tracey Brass Band in 1910, with spectators. In the 1950s Ernest Smithys was the band master and George and Michael Hydon played in the band.

The White Rose Orchestra in November 1908 preparing for their carnival performance. It must have taken a lot of work to make all the uniforms and the instruments!

Bovey women and children outside 'The Bell' ready for an outing.

E. G. Snell's local workmen ready for a works outing, outside the Old Dartmoor Inn in Dolphin Square. Mr Snell is the tall man on the back row, fourth from the left and Dave Lewis is sixth from the left. Snell's was where the Dartmoor garage is now and was a large builders firm.

An early view of a man and hounds outside the Dolphin Hotel and posting house with onlookers. The sign in the background is advertising the Dolphin Hotel Mews and horses and coaches for Dartmoor excursions and 'mourning' coaches.

The hunt in Union Square outside the Union Hotel (now the Cromwell Arms).

Bovey children in fancy dress walking down Fore Street in 1953.

THIS SHIP IS NOT TO BE USED BY BOYS OVER 10 YEARS OLD. H.A. BENTINCK

THE NEW PLEASURE GROUNDS. BOVEY TRACEY. No. 900.

The New Pleasure Grounds. This playground was situated where Station Road car park is now. The sign next to the 'Ship' must have been tough for the boys! The playground moved to Mill Marsh Park in the 1970s and the new play equipment is now open to all children under 12!

BRITISH LEGION CARNIVAL.
AUG 21st 1948. 1st PRIZE.

The Parish Church of St Peter, St Paul and St Thomas of Canterbury's entry in the British Legion Carnival in 1948 with their Olympic float. First Prize, XIV Olympiad. It is amazing to think that 64 years after this picture was taken London is about to host the Olympics again in 2012!

Bovey Cycle Club in 1901 in Union Square outside the Union Hotel. There is still a cycling club in Bovey Tracey today.

St John's Association football team in around 1910. The earliest recorded game was in 1899. Around 1950 there was a merger of the Bovey St John's team with the Bovey Town team. The current Bovey Tracey Football Club remains popular with three senior and eight junior teams.

Bovey Tracey cricket team in the early 1920s. Founded c.1850 the current cricket club at the Recreation Ground has three men's teams who compete in the Devon Cricket League and a women's team. The club also encourages many local young people to get involved in cricket.

Bovey Bowling Club members in 1913. Established in 1911, the Club was originally known as the Bovey Tracey Cricket and Bowling Club and originally shared the cricket pavilion until the mid 1970s. A new Bowling Club pavilion was opened in 2008.

Bovey Tracey Charter Celebrations with cars crossing Bovey bridge in 1960. In 2010 the town celebrated 750 years since the granting of the market and Charter to the town. There was a parade through the town and many events and celebrations in Mill Marsh Park.

CHAPTER 5

STREETS AND BUILDINGS GREAT AND SMALL

There are over a hundred buildings of special architectural or historical interest in Bovey Tracey and the surrounding area, these are all listed and part of the town's very valuable and diverse heritage. Although at first glance some of these streets are still similar, look more closely and see how Bovey has changed over the years.

A previously unseen early photograph of Bradley Ford Tollhouse cottage from the 1890s. This was situated on the bend on the road leading out of Bovey, round Bradley Bends to Chudleigh Knighton and Exeter. This corner is known locally as Bumpsie Berry Corner after a man who was killed there.

Coombe Cross in the 1950s with a view looking towards the Parish Church, with mostly fields where Coombe Close is now!

The large house to the left of the Parish Church is now known as Church Style, Bradley Road. In the south wall of the garden near to Trough Lane there is an important granite trough and recess. It is known locally as St Mary's Well, and part of the Ashwell spring used to flow here.

The current Church Hill House at 58 East Street on the corner of Trough Lane dates from around 1851. In 1881 a Mrs Loveys ran a girls' boarding school here. In World War Two the house was requisitioned as a sergeants' billet and a soldier accidentally fired a bullet through the ceiling, narrowly missing a man in the room above!

A view of East Street looking towards the Parish Church around 1907. The house on the left is No 50, 'Bell House.' It is late sixteenth century or early seventeenth century. It has a large early nineteenth century glazed door with 12 panes at the front. It was the original Bell Inn.

The Manor House on East Street is a late medieval manor house built about 1200. It was enlarged in the early or mid nineteenth century and was a guest house at one time. William De Tracey is said to have lived in the Manor house and later added his name to Bovey, so renaming the town.

A postcard view up East Street towards the Church dated 1960 with Horrell's Dairy on the left. Mr Horrell was a dairyman and had a horse and cart and delivered milk to Chudleigh Knighton, Heathfield, Brimley and parts of Bovey. The next house beyond the dairy was the Liberal Club.

A view of Bovey Tracey Town Hall, Town Hall Place in about 1911. It was built in 1865 at a cost of £1300. The hall was originally used for vestry meetings, balls and concerts. The original entrance with steps leading up to it can be seen on the west side of the building.

FORE STREET, BOVEY TRACEY   Fredman's Series   25850

This early postcard of Union Square is from before 1897, as there is no Jubilee Fountain which was erected to commemorate Queen Victoria's Diamond Jubilee. In June 2012 Bovey had celebrations for Queen Elizabeth II's Diamond Jubilee, the second monarch to achieve this!

Fore Street, Bovey Tracey.

An early postcard view of Fore Street from Union Square in the early twentieth century. Mann and Son, butchers and Alford and Son, ladies and gents tailors are the shops on the right. The tall building in the centre was the Constitutional Club, notice the large clock at the top.

A later view from Union Square looking down Fore Street with one car! On the right is A.E. Collins motors and cycle shop and next to it is the Co-operative Society. On the left is Simon May's watchmakers, now Tesco's, then National and Provincial Bank, Mann's and then Co-op drapery.

The old Riverside Nurseries at the bottom of Fore Street was run by Mr May. The nursery used to provide cut flowers, bedding plants, bouquets and wreaths. In 1956 wreaths cost two pounds and ten shillings!

An early photograph of Parke View which stands at the bottom of Fore Street on the corner of Parkelands. Originally part of the Parke Estate the house had stables and large orchards and a conservatory. There were no other houses built nearby and just fields in the foreground!

A rare view of Mary Street looking towards the town. The houses on the left are still there! The first houses on the right were demolished for the car park. The next cottages were burnt down in 1937 and rebuilt after the war. The Methodist chapel in the distance on the far right is also gone.

Cromwells Way was built around 1948. The bases were known as 'Cornish Units' which were made from china clay waste and built by SNW contractors from Cornwall. The upper part of the building made of timber was added by Heath Brothers. Costain's builders built the road.

"WOLLEIGH," BOVEY TRACEY. S. DEVON

Wolleigh House is situated off the Moretonhampstead Road. It was built in stone in the Gothic style in the 1890s by Henry Tanner Ferguson, and it originally had 75 acres of land. Henry was a railway engineer and he and his wife Beatrice had eight children and moved from 'Plumley.'

Cross Cottage was built in the mid 1770s and takes its name from the small stone cross placed near the entrance in the garden wall on the south side of Moretonhampstead Road. A Dr. Croker lived here in the early 1800s. His daughter Annie set up the British School on Mary Street.

Station Road, Bovey Tracey.

CANN, PHOTO.

A postcard of Station Road from the bridge around the 1890s. The cottage in the foreground on the left was owned by a Mr and Mrs Dear and is no longer there. The Old Dolphin can be seen further along the road on the left, which was then a butcher's shop run by William Bovey.

The Bridge, Bovey Tracey

Published by Edwards, Bovey, Devon.

This early postcard shows the building beside the bridge known as the Mill, built in 1854 by Mr John Divett. A wheel pumped water across to his house at Riverside. On the left is a distant view of a tall chimney on lower Fore Street, further research is needed to clarify what this was?

Old Folks at Home, Bovey Tracey.

This postcard shows an elderly couple outside the front of Marsh Cottages dated 1908. Five families originally lived in the cottages.

This photograph provides a rare and unique view of Marsh Cottages around the 1900s with the Mill behind them. The Cottages were situated between the river and Marsh Path, and were demolished around the time of World War One.

Blenheim Terrace built around 1905 with the railway in the foreground. It received some damage during the Second World War when a German pilot strafed the railway line. One house has a different bay window because the front of the house had to be rebuilt.

A postcard dated 1910 showing Heathfield Terrace on Newton Road with some young girls standing in the road. The Bovey Tracey tollhouse can just be seen in the distance on the right and is surrounded by fields.

Marlborough Terrace was built in 1904 on land owned by Major Hole. The larger house on the corner of Marlborough Terrace, nearest the traffic island, was used as a hospital for a while and was later a hotel and provided bed and breakfast.

A view of the Dolphin Hotel taken around 1913. A carriage and horses can just be seen facing towards the Moor ready for an outing.

These houses were built on Brimley Road around 1900 and as the postcard shows there was open countryside all around!

These houses on Pottery Road were built for workers from the Bovey Tracey Pottery. This rare postcard is dated 1920 and shows Mr Harris the dairyman and poulterer with his horse and cart and a dog in the foreground.

Indio (Indeo) is thought to have originally been a priory. The first pottery and porcelain production in Bovey Tracey was established on this site in 1766 by Nicholas Crisp. William Cookworthy the Plymouth chemist also carried out early porcelain experiments here.

St Mary's was built in 1873, and in 1881 owned by Adela Divett the daughter of the then Pottery owner. In 1894 Canon Courtenay owned it and left it to his niece Agnes. In 1933 it was rented to the Church Army who later bought it, and in 1999 it was sold and divided into houses.

This rare wedding photograph of Emily Laetitia Parlby and William Robert Hole and their guests outside Parke House in 1875 is the earliest photograph in this book. The current house was built in 1825 and is now the administrative headquarters of Dartmoor National Park.

Bovey Tracey Tollhouse (Newton Bushell), on the Newton Road, dates from around 1826. In the 1841 census it is listed as 'Turnpike House' and Richard Bully, a shoemaker lived there with his family. Once known as the Tollhouse at 'Towns End' there is still a Town's End Cottage.

Chapter 6

Schools and Hospitals

Small schools were started in various places around Bovey. There was originally a grammar school on Fore Street which then moved up to where the Edgemoor Hotel is now. The churches set up schools. The St John's Infant School started in around 1874 and there was also the British School on Mary Street. Brimley School was on a site near Prestbury Court and Miss Bodkin's kindergarten was at Indio Lodge. The Bovey Primary School originally known as the Council School was built on Abbey Road in 1911.

A small school was built in Heathfield in 1898 for Candy and Co children.

Various houses were used as small hospitals before the opening of the Cottage hospital in 1931. St John's Cottage Hospital was started at 7, Heathfield Terrace (then part of Heathfield), 'Revelstoke' on Mary Street and Marlborough House on the corner of Marlborough Terrace.

The large Hawkmoor Sanitorium on the Moretonhampstead Road was built in 1913 for patients with tuberculosis.

A postcard of the British School football team dated 1908. The British School (now the Gospel Hall) opened in around 1866 at a cost of £700 and was run by Annie Croker who campaigned against the high church philosophy of the time.

GEO. W. HOLDEN, CARDIFF, PLYMOUTH & JOHANNESBURG, S.A.
PHOTOGRAPHIC ARTIST. MANAGER

The British School children and teacher in 1902. The building was not big enough and there were so many children that an annexe in a wooden hut was used at the bottom of Spion Kop. The British School eventually closed in 1911.The building on Mary Street is now the Gospel Hall.

Boys and their teachers at the Church School, which was opposite the Parish Church of St Peter, St Paul and St Thomas. Set up in around 1834, it had the best attendance in the area. In 1868 the boys moved across into what is now the Parish Church Rooms followed by the girls in 1884.

Ye Olde Yew Tree House later called Holly Tree House on Fore Street, originally comprised three thatched cottages. The porch dates back to the fifteenth century. The first grammar school (Endowed School) started here around 1713. Adjoining the Endowed School was an orchard known as School House Orchard. This was sold in 1854.

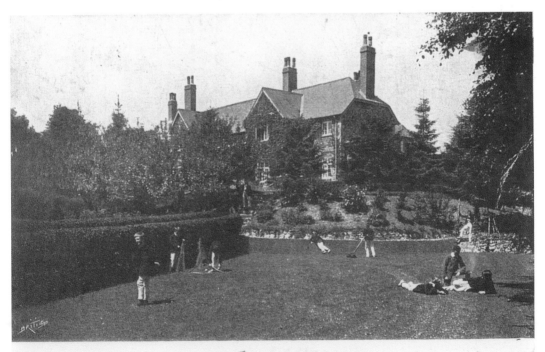

Elliott & Fry,   THE LAWN, BOVEY TRACEY SCHOOL.   London, W.

Bovey Tracey Grammar School on Haytor Road, (now the Edgemoor Hotel). The building was on a site given by Mr Hole and used to educate 25 boys aged 7-16, from 1879 to 1908.

An old photograph of girls gardening at Bovey Primary School around 1920, before the building of Priory, supervised by their teacher Mr Bint. In 2011 the school celebrated their centenary and a host of events took place to mark this special occasion. A commemorative tree was planted; a reminder of the past and symbolic of the future of education in our community. The school currently has 302 children.

Bovey Tracey Primary School children with instruments in the 1950's.

The foundation stone for Bovey Hospital was laid in 1931 by Violet Wills and the Cottage Hospital was completed in 1932 at a cost of around £4,000. It had wards for men and women and an operating theatre. The hospital is still in use today.

At the top of Mary Street just below the Hospital are Croker's Alms Houses. Built in 1929 they were erected from a bequest in the will of Samuel Croker on land given in the memory of Dr Arthur Storrs. The Tracey Alms Houses are situated at 35-43 East Street and were built in 1910.

Hawkmoor Sanitorium was a large establishment built in 1913 on the Moretonhampstead Road on the western edge of the town to care for patients with tuberculosis. This early picture shows wooden huts which were swivelled to follow the sun and patients were given plenty of fresh air!

The Sanitorium had its own chapel designed by Dr J. C. Smyth and built by staff and patients. The stained glass window shows Christ healing the sick and when the Hospital was demolished, St Luke's chapel was incorporated into one of the new houses on the site.

A sketch of the Matron's house which was in the grounds of the Hawkmoor Sanitorium. Originally this grand building was the estate house and had an orangery. Matron was in charge of all the nursing staff and did a daily ward round and each ward sister had to give a report!

51465. Hawkmoor Chest Hospital, Bovey Tracey.

The surgical wing at Hawkmoor. In the late 1950s with the arrival of mass radiography and antibiotics, tuberculosis was being diagnosed early and cured and the demand for beds fell. The Hospital closed in 1975 and new houses were built on the site known as Hawkmoor Park.

The old Primary School, Heathfield in the early 1990's. The building is on Little Bovey Lane near the railway and was built by public subscription in 1898 to educate the nearby Candy and Co workers' children and closed in 2005.

St Catherine's Church of England Nursery and Primary School moved to its new site on Musket Road, Heathfield in September 2005. The school began a United Schools Federation with St Michael's, Kingsteignton in 2011. There are currently 146 full time and 29 part time children.

Chapter 7

Transport

One of the most striking aspects of the majority of these early views is that they show deserted streets compared to the multitude of cars of today! Methods of transport were very different then as this chapter clearly shows. The building of the railway brought better transport links for Bovey Pottery and other local industry as well as providing a regular supply of tourists wanting to get away from the big city and down to Devon to enjoy some fresh Dartmoor air.

John Knapman Harris and family behind the Bell Inn with a new bike! He used to make as well as repair shoes and hang the shoes outside his house for sale! His daughter Elizabeth Ann married William Thompson in 1893, who was a cycle maker in Torquay and later in Bovey.

Members of the Rugby Club ready for a visit to Dartmoor on a horse drawn carriage around 1895. The Union Hotel together with the Dolphin and Railway Hotels provided coaches with 4 horses which were used to take visitors on popular tours of Dartmoor.

A coach and horses and coachman with passengers taking part in the Mary Street Carnival.

1931 'Grandpa' Jim Fouracre leading a horse with a beautifully decorated carnival float!

A Great Western Railway parcel delivery from Bovey Station on the Brimley Road opposite the cricket pavilion, and some boys hitching a ride around 1910, outside the house called 'Milverton' which is now converted into flats.

G. W. Railway Station, Bovey Tracey.

A view of Bovey Station at around the beginning of the twentieth century showing the arrival of a train from Newton Abbot. Built in 1866 the railway ran for nearly a century until the passenger service was withdrawn on 2nd March 1959. The building is now the Heritage Centre.

An AEC charabanc parked at Bovey Station in 1926 ready to take visitors up to the Moors. By the mid 1930s in the summer months there were eleven trains a day between Newton Abbot and Moretonhampstead and seven between Newton Abbot and Bovey for all the many visitors!

Moir and Davie, Central Garage, Motor Engineers was on Dolphin Square at the end of the Newton Road next to the Dartmoor Hotel. At a much later date in 1958 they also hired coaches and it cost £2.10 shillings for coach hire! The telephone number was just '10'!

Interior of Moir and Davie garage, Dolphin Square with a number of cars needing a service. Mr Moir and Mr Davie were brothers in law.

An early picture of Dartmoor Motor Works and garage in Dolphin Square.

Charabanc outing outside Hodges the Hairdressers, Union Square in the early twentieth century.

Car in the floods outside the Old Dolphin on Station Road. Bovey is known to have had occasional floods in the past in the Station Road area in winter storms.

No 16 Bus in Union Square leaving for Newton Abbot. The Electricity shop is on the left.

Bovey Tracey Parish Council's first fire engine. Originally it was kept at the Town Hall. The Fire Station is now next to Station Road roundabout, and staffed by the Devon and Somerset Fire and Rescue service.

A Pickfords truck getting stuck at Town Hall Place by the Town Hall. A familiar story as this still happens today with big lorries.

CHAPTER 8

HOTELS, GUEST HOUSES, PUBS AND CAFES

Bovey Tracey known as one of the 'gateways to the moor' has always been a popular holiday destination due to its excellent location being situated on the edge of magnificent Dartmoor and within easy reach of the beautiful South Devon coast.

Writing postcards while on holiday was always a popular way of sending messages home to family and friends. It is surprising to find that there are over 400 different postcards of Bovey Tracey alone! A postcard provides a snapshot in time and the messages are often interesting too. I still try to send postcards when I go away to keep this tradition going.

A postcard view of the Dolphin and Railway Hotels in Dolphin Square, dated 1910.

COOMBE CROSS HOTEL, BOVEY TRACEY

The Coombe Cross Hotel on Coombe Lane was started in 1952 by Elizabeth and Anne Hebditch who organised various activity holidays. It was sold it in 1984 and it is still a hotel to this day.

SUMMERFIELD BOARDING HOUSE, BOVEY TRACEY, MRS COOMBE, PROPRIETRESS.

Summerfield Boarding House on East Street. Originally two seventeenth century cottages known as Coniam's tenements, it had a yard, pound house, cider cellar, gardens and large orchards and was bought by Dr Hayden in 1854. The rent was 1 shilling and 8 pence!

Front House Lodge, East Street. In 1646 Oliver Cromwell and some of his Roundhead soldiers surprised a contingent of Wentworth's army playing cards at Front House Lodge. Wentworth's troops caused a distraction to expedite their escape by throwing coins out of the window!

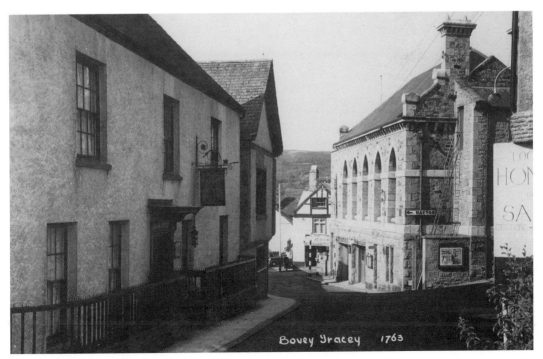

A view down East Street with Front House Lodge and the Town Hall in 1950 with Dartmoor in the distance. The advertisement on the Town Hall is for the latest cinema release being shown there, which was the Western film 'Rio Grande' staring John Wayne and Maureen O'Hara!

View from the top of Fore Street in 1907. The Town Cross with Ellicott's Bell Inn behind it and Cann's the shop next to it. It was later Tregoning's shop then the British Monument Café and Tudor Café and is where the Chinese takeaway restaurant is now.

A later view of The Bell Inn, Town Hall Place with the Fruit Shop and Dart's dairy next to it. The old entrance to the Town Hall is also visible on the left with the walled steps and doorway. From 1929 to1966 the Bell was run by Jimmy and Flo Netley. Flo was the first woman town councillor.

In 1881 The King of Prussia Inn on Upper Fore St was run by Elizabeth Lavis and her descendants still live in Bovey. Claude Prowse ran the pub for 30 years from 1917 and was renowned for keeping the skeleton of a dead cat under the counter!

A group of men outside the Heavitree Arms, previously known as the King of Prussia Inn, before an outing. It was a traditional pub offering fine real ales and a beer garden. It reverted to its original name before it closed in around 2008.

Union Hotel and Post Office,   Bovey Tracey.   E 31661

The Cromwell Arms was originally a row of tenement houses and site of an apple yard and brew house. It was an inn called the Lamb in 1777 and later the Dartmoor Inn and in the 1880s was known as the Union Hotel and owned by the Wolfinden family. The old post office is on the right.

The Union Square from Fore Street, Bovey Tracey.

The Union Hotel in the 1950s, Union Square. S. E. Collins garage and cycle shop is on the left and was situated where Lloyds the chemist is now.

The Riverside Private Hotel in the 1960s had large tea gardens backing onto the river and was open to non residents. Now the Riverside Inn. It is hard to envisage now that Fore Street was the main road through Bovey, as of course Le Molay Littry Way was not built until the 1980s.

Originally a coaching house, the Old Dolphin dates back to around 1625 and due to frequent flooding the landlord decided to build the new Dolphin Hotel in the 1880s. In recent years it became a pub and was renamed the Old Thatched Inn. It was badly damaged by fire in 2008.

The Railway Hotel on Dolphin Square was built by J.G. Beer in the 1860s. Convenient for visitors, it was close to the newly built railway station. There used to be a ballroom, and gardens at the back with fruit trees and chickens. There was a bad fire there in the 1920s.

A later postcard of the Dartmoor Hotel, originally the Railway Hotel, dated 1941. In around 2006 it was converted into houses. The building to the left has been demolished and new houses erected on Bowden's Close.

The Dolphin Hotel on Dolphin Square was built in the 1880s and owned by John Joll. The ballroom upstairs originally had its own dance band, the 'Dolphins'. There used to be large stables here and horse drawn carriages would leave for trips to Dartmoor.

The Torvue Café was built around 1910 on Station Road close to the level crossing and used to serve passengers from the nearby railway station. It is now a tearooms and bed and breakfast and renamed the Copper Kettle, and is close to Station Road roundabout.

The Blenheim Country House Hotel, now a private house, was situated on the corner of Chapple Road and Brimley Road. Notice the great views of Dartmoor with no other buildings nearby. Further up Brimley Road there was also the Prestbury Court Hotel which is now a nursing home.

Edymead Hotel, Bovey Tracey.

The Edymead Hotel close to the Blenheim Hotel is now converted into flats and known as Brimley Court. Francis Galton, a cousin of Darwin stayed here. He is noted for genetic experiments with sweet peas and for the first fingerprint classification system!

The Edgemoor Hotel on Haytor Road was originally built as Bovey Tracey grammar school. The house was later known as Edgehill Boarding Establishment, and then became The Edgehill Hotel and later the name was altered to 'Edgemoor' Private Hotel.

COLEHAYES PARK HOTEL
HAYTOR ROAD
BOVEY TRACEY
DEVON

Colehayes started as a small residence in around 1540. The Haytor Dartmoor granite tramway and Bovey Pottery leat used to run through this 400 acre estate. The current Georgian house was a private residence until 1952 and has since been used as a hotel and field studies centre.

Brookside tea gardens in 1945. Originally it was a private house owned by Mr Wyatt. Cream teas and homemade scones were a speciality and bed and breakfast was also available. The new building opened in 2002, the original site was where Brook Close houses are now.

A postcard of the Clarendon Guest House on Newton Road, dated 1908. It still provided bed and breakfast accommodation until recently. It is a red bricked, double bay fronted Victorian semi detached house. It is situated just before the end of Newton Road where it meets Station Road.

CHAPTER 9

HEATHFIELD

Originally 'Bovey Heathfield' was much larger and extended right up to Bovey Tracey. The views in this chapter show the railway as well as workers and buildings associated with Candy and Co in the early twentieth century.

Candy & Company Ltd, which in its early days traded as 'The Great Western Potteries Brick Tile and Clay Works' was founded in the early 1870s by Frank Candy.

It was a very extensive brickworks, making fire bricks, paving bricks and sanitary ware. The company launched an art pottery in January 1923 producing a range of Art Deco designs. The new pottery named 'Westcontree Ware' was very colourful, and was a distinctive 'decorative pottery of speciality glaze effects'. In 1937 the pottery was known as 'Candy ware' . The pottery continued until it closed in the late 1950s.

Station staff posing for the camera outside Heathfield Signal Box around 1930. The signal box was built in 1916, using white Candy bricks and had a hipped roof of grey slate and contained 58 levers! It was at the far end of the 'up' platform by the junction for the Teign Valley Line.

A good view of Heathfield Station and the factory of Candy & Co as a train arrives from Moretonhampstead hauled by an unidentified '2161' class 2-6-2T running bunker first, about 1906. The signal box at this time was closer to the station building.

Candy and Company Ltd workers in the early part of the twentieth century. There were around 570 men employed at the works in the 1930s. In the 1960s the company changed its name to Candy Tiles Ltd. In 1998 it became known as 'British Ceramic Tile' (BCT).

THE "DEVON" FIRE

COSIEST AND BEST OF ALL

PLACED FIRST in recent OFFICIAL TESTS of Domestic Fires carried out in the NEW GOVERNMENT OFFICES jointly by H.M. OFFICE OF WORKS and the Smoke Abatement Society.

Consumption of fuel and production of smoke each one-quarter less than the average of 36 competing grates.

Easily fixed to existing mantelpieces.

Supplied in a large variety of designs to suit any room and any style of building.

Highest Awards and Medals awarded by the Royal Sanitary Institute at the 1906, Bristol, and the 1907, South Kensington, Exhibitions.

An advertising postcard for 'The Devon Fire,' Cosiest and Best of All! This card was sent in January 1909 from Candy and Company's London showroom at 87 Newman St, Oxford St. In the early 1960s bathroom and kitchen tiles became popular and replaced the fireplace tiles.

A mission meeting at Candy and Company Ltd. A visiting evangelist Frank Penfold talking to Candy workers from his car in the 1920s. Rev J. Windsor is the man on the left of the car.

Heathfield 'Tin' Church was an iron Chapel of Ease built in the late nineteenth century to seat 60 persons and was situated next to the old Primary School on Little Bovey Lane in Heathfield.

Mrs Mary Jane Polyblank in 1910, outside the crossing keeper's cottage on the Teign Valley line, which was positioned just after Heathfield Station. 'Haytor View' cottages can be seen in the background. The cottage has since been demolished, but some of the track is still visible!

Brow Hill Estate's houses were built around 1930 for the managers of the nearby Candy and Company Ltd Brick works.

Moorland View. These houses are on the Old Newton Road and were also built for workers from the Candy and Company Ltd brick works. The post office was also in one of these houses at one time.

Heathfield Post Office at 'Candy Cottages', there was also a Telegraph Office and shop. These cottages were built for workers from Candy and Company in the 1880s. There used to be a wooden footbridge at the southern end of the road providing access across the railway to work.

GENERAL VIEW HEATHFIELD POST OFFICE   H 1402

Heathfield Post Office around 1950 was situated at the end of the Old Newton Road at the junction with the A38. This building was recently demolished and new houses are now built in its place.